SHOW UP CONFIDENT

THE NEW WAY TO GET READY FOR YOUR DAY AND YOUR LIFE

MICHELE CHARLES GUSTAFSON

HUE AND STYLE® PRESS

Dedication

I dedicate this work to:

My Daughter and Niece

May you grow your gifts into talents every day and use them to find joy, independence, and freedom.

Make your mark changing lives with your confidence.

My Parents

Thank you for giving me the spark that taught me to use my gifts.

Your legacy lives in those I've changed.

In my handwriting, I express my Meaningful Outcome.
For those I touch and teach with my words, work, life, and
legacy I offer:

~ MCG.

Contents

READ THIS! MY GIFT TO YOU!

Congratulations on buying this book, I would like to gift you an audiobook preview 100% FREE!

TO DOWNLOAD GO TO

https://www.hueandstyle.com/show-up-confident-audiobook

Discover the new way to transform your confidence, starting with how you get ready for your day.

Even if you've been overwhelmed, stuck in a rut or tried every "tip" in the book, you CAN crack the code and learn to turn how you present yourself into a self-propelling motivator and magnetic tool for your next success. It starts with something you might not expect.

START NOW

Sign up and get a powerfully simple *FREE* companion resource for your book that prepares you to increase your value, voice, and visibility with your image & confidence:

https://www.hueandstyle.com/show-up-confident-free

THE INTENTION

This is not about clothes, but about dressing in self-acceptance.
This is not about fashion, but about styling your life's intention.

This is about
Honoring yourself with a confidence that is
Renewing,
Energizing,
& Preparing – You.

This is about
Illuminating your life with a confidence that is
Beautifying,
Strengthening,
& Liberating – You.

With acceptance of yourself,
With intention for your life,
You become a force of greatness –

Every day you show up confident.

Let's jump in.

~MCG.

Section I

RENEW

THE JOURNEY

"It's never a bad idea to choose yourself first." ~ MCG.

Confidence is slippery and sticky at the same time. Here's why.

Confidence is a sureness of feeling about something—yourself, your circumstances, or your abilities—and feelings change.

Your confidence will be slippery when you become disconnected from feeling certain. When you lose confidence in one area of your life, it slips from others, making your decisions harder, choices rougher, and direction less focused. If you've ever gone hiking on a gravel path up a hill with flip flops instead of hiking boots, you've felt this. You take a step but can't get traction. You feel unstable and it takes you longer to get where you're going.

The flip side is when you stay connected to your confidence; it gets sticky. It adheres to every part of your life and binds them together. With the right hiking boots, with nubby grip, you can take steady steps with sure footing and you can enjoy the view instead of focusing on the rough path. Renewing confidence by shifting how you see yourself in life (and in the mirror too) creates a power that flows into the decisions, choices, and direction in the rest of life. This is the new way!

While confidence is usually associated with skill or achievement, I've learned that the strongest, swiftest new confidence comes from somewhere else.

Confidence comes from finishing.

Think about your confidence. How would you describe it right now? Is it slippery or sticky in your life? If it's slippery, that's ok. It happens to all of us multiple times in our lives. My aim is to take you on a journey that renews you, energizes you, and prepares you to show up more confident every day.

Over my decades helping women develop their confidence—no matter which area they focused on, growing their self-assuredness, their business venture, marketing themselves, or dressing themselves, when they began to complete (finish) steps in their journey, they created momentum.

Believe me, this momentum you create by seeing yourself inside and out as who you are becoming creates a confidence that gets sticky really fast leading to new breakthroughs, new adventures, and new successes.

Finishing any worthy journey doesn't happen overnight. It takes time and preparation. To prepare yourself for this journey, and to get the most from this book and our time together, you will need four essentials.

1. A Travel Companion

This is no one other than your truest, inner self (soul, spirit, essence). Attune yourself to your essence and you will have a guide for every step with whispers of directions, insights, and comforting encouragements. The best way to activate this unwavering self-support is to learn to open a new conversation with yourself.

2. A Journal

I know, I know, you may want to resist the idea of journaling with reasons like, "I don't know what to write" or "I don't have time" or "I just can't get into it." For almost all of those reasons, and for all the years I've helped women develop a journaling practice, those reasons come up because you're not connected to the aim of journaling. Your aim is to start, nurture, and continue a conversation with yourself that starts to feel like a trusted friendship over time after regular conversation. You will also need a favorite pen or two.

3. Time

The most valuable time you'll spend is with yourself. Give yourself the gift of time to read, pause, reflect, and journal with the opportunities I offer you at each step. Choose your favorite time of day where you can be free with your thoughts and use the prompts I offer to explore your thoughts in the sections called "Reflection and Journal Work" spaced out over "Today," "Tomorrow," and "The Next Day." Use this spacing or take more.

4. Effort

Intention powers miracles. Give yourself the gift of clear intention for this journey. Why are you here? What is your aim? Clarity with this will power how you take your first steps and will drive your efforts to find new insights.

Remember this is all a journey. Let's take it little by little, day by day. This is all part of the transformation. For all journeys, the joy is in walking the steps, not arriving at the destination. Now that you are ready, enjoy your steps.

REFLECTIONS & JOURNAL WORK

TODAY: Reflect on why the journey to "show up confident" holds significance in your life right now. For what would you use renewed confidence to energize in your life?

What are you preparing for next that requires your most powerful self?

TOMORROW: Explore your reaction to starting a new conversation with yourself by journaling.

Does it excite you or make you nervous? Why?

THE NEXT DAY: Free write. Talk to yourself about anything that is coming up for you about this journey. Gift yourself three pages of a judgment-free journal-filling conversation.

2

THE BEAUTY OF CHANGE

_____

"Evolution is the only thing that's permanent." ~ MCG.

The sun was shining into the skinny windows on either side of the hospital bed on the morning of February 28, 2002. The heart rate monitor beeped with falsely comforting regularity. The pale yellow glow of the sun streaming in mixed with the ivory-green walls of the private room put a sickly tint in the room that seemed to foreshadow that something was happening today. My heart hung in my chest; my stomach soured as I leaned over the bed.

This is the day my Dad would leave the planet.

I was with him at his bedside when he passed. Together with my sister and husband, we watched as doctors shuffled in and out all day with a heaviness. We watched the nurse turn the heart monitor away and then off. Her eyes welled up as she looked at us and shook her head with the confirmation of "no more."

That was the event that changed everything. Everything that happened after that minute and in the years and decades to come was in some way related to that incomparable pivot. I was twenty-four years old. His passing changed how I saw life, how I navigated loss, how I discovered purpose, how I expressed meaning and ultimately how I would come to serve others.

While in the moment of change, sadness, grief, and unbearable loss—there are gifts too.

My dad's passing made me see how many confidence lessons I'd received from the honor of having him in my life. He taught me how to find new hope and confidence after any difficult situation.

Maybe you've gone through incomparable pivots too, or maybe you're going through one now. Scan your life. Was it a passing or a divorce? Was it a diagnosis or even a recovery? Each pivot is an opportunity to find new personal power.

Lessons I learned from my dad on building confidence:

- "Be Sharp as a Tack"

  You honor yourself when you care about how you present yourself. This honor shines. People want to be around you, and with that connection you can serve them and do your greatest work. Satisfaction and joy in your life follows.

- "Speak Up"

  No mumbling. Use your voice. Say what you know and own it.

- "Your Work Is Service"

  What you do in your life is meant to help someone else become more of themselves. No matter what you choose to do, see it as a service to others and give it with excellence.

I found healing in living out these lessons which shifted into purposeful momentum to move past the paralysis that grief can bring.

My mom delivered her own set of lessons. She's a natural teacher, and she became my model of resilience and an example of how to take what life gives you and find grace, new resolve, and personal meaning for your next step.

Growing up as the last of ten children and as the daughter of a steel mine worker in small-town Pennsylvania, my mom learned to make the most happiness with her present condition of life. As a little girl, she found joy in her father making an old chicken coop into a playhouse. She painted it with leftover paint, and sewed curtains for the windows, and spent time feeling safe inside her little playhouse. Her ability to bounce-back from anything always centered on her ability to keep herself safe. This is what she taught me.

She told stories about standing up for herself to fend off playful roughhousing from her older brothers and punching out schoolyard boys for their unwanted advances. The common thread: always protecting herself with a mix of fearlessness and humor.

My dad's passing made me see how many resilience lessons I've received and used from having her as my mother.

Lessons I learned from my mom on building resilience:

- **"Learn Your Self-Defense"**

   You are the only one you can count on to keep yourself safe. Learn to defend yourself, but more importantly, stay aware of your surroundings, trust your intuition, and listen to it. When things don't seem right, you're right. When your gut whispers to you, listen.

- **"Find a new way and do it."**

   Beyond fear is something you're not sure you know how to do. Figure out what you don't think you know, find the right people for support, and be brave enough to do what feels uncomfortable.

- **"Figure out why you're here."**

You have a reason for being here. It's a simple reason, but a powerful one. Find it and live it and you won't work to be happy. You'll just be happy.

Resilience helps you find a way forward from anything. You have an opportunity to learn from the event of a change, and it gives you clues for how to become your best.

From my parents I got a foundation on how to reframe myself in the difficult, challenging, uncomfortable events of life. From Nina Simone I got the anthem for it. "Everything must change. Nothing stays the same." In her velvety voice, Nina reminded the entire gathering at my dad's funeral that, though uncomfortable, change is the only thing that is constant in our lives.

It's natural to want to avoid change, but if you can shift what it means to you, and for you, you can use it to evolve. You become your own recovery artist as you build bounce-back ability and new self-acceptance. To see the beauty in the end of a cycle and the beginning of a new one dissolves the torture about losing something and replaces it with a sense of adventure to move forward.

That juicy place of self-acceptance and adventure is the beauty of change. It's where you get to place time, energy, love, and attention on yourself to uncover renewed confidence and refreshed resilience. You get to be generous with your healing, to listen to the whispers of your heart, to hear the lessons of your life's adventures, to trust a new path, and to make choices that serve you. This is blissful and freeing.

3

THE ADVENTURE OF RESILIENCE

"Your beautiful new beginning starts with belief in your-self." ~MCG.

Change and transition are different. Think about "change" as "the event" and "transition" as "your response" after the event.

On a journey "change" is the stop sign at the intersection of your path. "Transition" is your decision to go left or right on the way to a destination that is important to you. Transition is the catalyst for building new resilience and new confidence. It asks you to do something new, develop new character, and to use your gifts, talents, virtues and values to create a new reality.

When I was eighteen, I decided to attend Queen's University. I lived two plane rides away in Alberta and to attend would need to commit to relocating to Ontario over 3, 000 kilometers away—across the country.

It was the beginning of an adventure in resilience. My conviction, desire, and determination to go to school there outweighed the unknowns that would take me out of my comfort zone. The unknowns tested me the first day I arrived and were my first of many lessons in the power of resilience.

I stepped off the Dash-8 prop plane and onto the tarmac of the tiny Kingston airport. As I walked toward the doors, preparing to claim my luggage, my chest tightened as I breathed in heavy, humid air. I thought, how the heck am I going to get my stuff to the dorm! I had landed with two 50+ pound suitcases and a 100+ pound travel trunk and needed to get it to a dorm I had never even seen before.

My mind raced, my heart raced faster, and I thought to myself, how do you fix this?

In my left ear and with more than a whisper, my mind answered the uneasiness in my gut. I heard it say, "You're going to need help. Reach out for people to help."

That "more than a whisper" message showed me the way. My eyes fell on a payphone that seemed to be divinely illuminated. I rushed to it, dialed "the people" at the school residency office. They arranged to have someone meet me when I arrived.

Perfect! Now, I just needed to get my 200+ pounds of my stuff over to the dorm.

I heard it again "Find the people."

Then I saw it! One lonely taxicab outside—a station wagon. No way! It would fit my stuff if I could get it before it left.

Heart raced again. I dashed outside leaving my things. To the middle-aged man filling out his logbook, I blurted out my plight and with a paternal smile that calmed my panic like a hug, he said, "Not to worry, Dear."

Relief mixed with a sense of accompaniment came over me. I did it. I figured it out and I had resolved it with that nudge to "find the people" and arrived at my dorm. This moving to school transition asked me to do, and learn, something new the very first day of the adventure. I'm sure you've had times that have felt like an adventure too.

If you embrace and focus on how you navigate a transition, instead of staying stuck at the event that starts it, you will see a wonderful opportunity for new self-trust and assuredness. It's not always easy to do when you're dealing with overwhelming emotion or massive unknowns but learning to see events as a balancing act of feeling, learning, and doing will bring out your best that is just below the surface.

Transition is the ultimate resilience builder and teaches you, event by event, quiet lessons that will serve your forward-moving journey. I got to develop my creativity, spirituality, and relationship skills with my move. I used the ability to trust my inner voice, look for ways to solve the problem, to ask for and accept help where I could have felt powerless. These are qualities I would use again and again. You can count on going through two to three transitions every decade of your life. You may go through them one at a time or you may experience two or three happening at once. Yikes. Common transitions can be:

- **Your relationship status:**

  Moving from single to a relationship, married to separated, separated to divorced, widowed, or new friendships to ending ones.

- **Your job or career:**

  A new position, a promotion, demotion, lay-off, the start of a business, a new partnership, or the close of a venture.

- **Your role:**

  Becoming a new parent, an active parent, an empty nester, a spouse or life partner, or a retiree.

- **Your health journey:**

  Being diagnosed, in-treatment, recovered, having body changes—up or down, mental health, pregnancy, or pregnancy loss.

- **Your major achievements or losses:**

Bucket-list milestones, the passing of a loved one, dreams won, anything lost.

Renewing your confidence and developing resilience after any change is a process of rediscovering, reevaluating, and realigning the importance of the priorities that make your life full and content. Life feels "hard" when you find yourself trying to force old priorities into new circumstances. Ease comes when you can discover the gift of an unexpected opportunity.

At any crossroad in your life, you have a new opportunity to evolve and be intentional about how you allocate your time, effort, energy and resources and to design a unique mix of life based on what is important to you at this new time.

Your life is made up of eleven elements that give meaning and purpose to your days and produce happiness and long-term satisfaction. All eleven areas experience a reshuffling after a change. Your ability to see the reshuffling in real-time helps you bounce-back and find new ways to cope, problem-solve, and find balance.

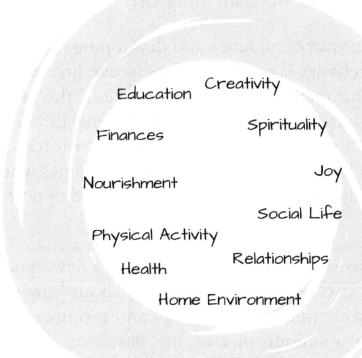

Assessing your priorities can happen in a split moment if you are attuned to it. I had to find a way, or make a way, to not be homeless my first day of university. I summoned some serious self-trust spirituality and creativity in those moments, but this assessment also happens over time—over days, weeks, or months. As I settled into a university environment where I knew no one, the change of a new school and living away from home tested all of my priorities in areas that eventually fell into a balance.

Falling in love with the practice of assessing your priorities helps you take a snapshot of what in your life is working (making you feel good, satisfied, accomplished, and fulfilled) and what is not working (what needs growth and attention). This practice of navigating, figuring out where the pieces belong, and deciding what to do next leads to standing up and out, working with purpose, and refreshing your entire outlook and outcomes.

REFLECTION AND JOURNAL WORK

TODAY: What change(s) has sparked a transition in the last six-twelve months?

Do you have more than one transition happening right now? In your journal—your safe space— write freely about how these changes and transitions have made you feel.

TOMORROW: Treat yourself to an exploration of your priorities. How have recent transitions affected them? On a scale of 1-10 (with one being the lowest, and ten being the highest) of happiness and satisfaction with each area, where do you sit?

1. Creativity – Your desire and ability to create something. Having and using your creativity helps you feel satisfied with anything you do. It's something we all have, though we may exercise it in different ways. Some use it to create art and beauty, others use it to create solutions. No matter how you use your creativity—it helps you do more, be more, and connect more with people and your world.
2. Spirituality – Your connection to, and relationship with, your higher self or a higher power or both as you define it. It's the closeness of the relationship to being and living in your essence and expressing it throughout your life.
3. Joy – Your unlimited feeling of giddy, blissful, contentment in the present moment.

4. Social Life – Your desire to be a part of a cherished community, and to actively offer yourself to it in a meaningful way.

5. Relationships – Your desire and ability to find, build, communicate in and nurture genuine, loving and supportive connections that feed your soul and fuel your growth.

6. Home Environment – Your physical surroundings that produce a sense of safety and security and express your definition of beauty.

7. Health – Your current state of physical and mental health and well-being.

8. Physical Activity – Your contentment with how you move and use your body for overall well-being.

9. Nourishment – Your desire and contentment with how you feed your body with food that helps you thrive.

10. Education – Your current state and desire to learn and acquire knowledge that supports your aims and purpose.

11. Finances – Your current relationship and practices toward how you use your financial

resources to take care of your life today and in the future.

THE NEXT DAY: Identify the top three areas you are happy with and the bottom three that need your attention. Keep these as you discover your next steps.

4

THE CONFIDENCE TO BELIEVE

"What you tell yourself in the quiet times, is the key to your success." ~ MCG.

When my sister and I were little, Disney's Dumbo came out on VHS. My dad insisted we watch it. I remember him rewinding the VHS tape over and over to a particular scene of the cartoon crows giving Dumbo a "magic feather" and telling him, "You have to bee-leee-ve you can fly." My Dad would stretch out the "believe" for emphasis and tap his forehead right between his eyes as he said it.

"You have to believe you can fly."

But how do you "believe" you can fly? (And where do you get your own magic feather, right?)

Confidence is having a sureness of self that you have what it takes to thrive in the important areas of your life. And remember, that starts with finishing.

After decades of mentoring women, I've seen that regardless of any judgment of an outcome—positive or negative, win or loss—with the right mindset, their desire and motivation to do more grew because they saw each "finish" as an opportunity to learn more about themselves, their journey, and their life. When you get acquainted with your current mindset and understand how it's either blocking or helping your ability to see what is meant for you, you'll know why you do or do not take action.

For the longest time, I wanted to be an architect. Designing something from the imagination, putting it on paper, showing connections, associations, detailing how structures relate to each other and knowing this "map" is used to build something into reality was fascinating. I abandoned that career dream after I found out how much math was involved, but I continued loving the metaphor of an architect's blueprint as a parallel for your mindset.

The foundation of your mindset is built on beliefs which are the brain's "shortcuts" for how you do life. You have beliefs about yourself that come from your history, family, upbringing, your inner greatest hurts and your grandest joys. You also have beliefs that have developed from the people, places and life experiences outside yourself. Beliefs form from times we needed to heal and when we wanted to celebrate—from experiences of both pain and joy. All rolled together, your beliefs influence your understanding of how, and why, life plays out as it does. They are your brain's shortcuts for how to stay safe, for how you create good and avoid bad as it makes a map of how you as a person relates to the big wide world.

Throughout your life, this blueprint of beliefs—your mindset—is quietly, automatically calling up these "shortcut" conclusions anytime you need to make a decision. Presumably, saving your time and avoiding any pain. Beliefs work for you as long as they are healthy and aligned with helping you grow as a person—improving how you think and feel about your importance, how you value yourself and your positive contribution to others. Beliefs can also hold you back. If during times of past transition, you developed beliefs that don't serve where you want to currently go, they can trap you into habits that are familiar but stagnating. You might feel like you're stuck or like you're not moving ahead as fast as you want. It's not always about skills you don't own, it's a mindset block. When this "feeling stuck" happens, it's an opportunity to look at where your foundation of beliefs needs to evolve.

I can't count the number of clients I've had who have struggled to lose weight and when they began working with me and came to realize that their weight loss was not about the skill of eating the right foods or exercising enough, it was about what they thought of themselves. One client, Olivia, had a mindset tape that played "Who do I think I am?" that told her she didn't deserve to stand out or to be the "go-to" leader to her own clients. When we uncovered, dismantled, and replaced this unserving belief with one that affirmed her purpose to give a safe space for others to own their worth, she shifted how she treated herself while she excelled at serving others. She lost over 18 lbs within a few months of working in my mentorship and gained national recognition in her relationship coaching business as a rising star. Beliefs are everything.

My Dad's Dumbo performance is part of my mindset blueprint. "You have to believe you can fly." Early in my entrepreneurial career, I set a mantra based on this belief. For my mission as a person and for my life it was simply, "to give confidence away." I let this phrase run every choice I made. If a job didn't achieve this aim, I didn't take it. If a volunteer opportunity didn't somehow produce this outcome, I said no to it. This four-word phrase was the expression of how I wished to relate to the world—it became how I presented myself, showed up, and took action. Here's why:

Beliefs Lead Behavior

In psychology, the behavior cycle illustrates how you make decisions and follow through. The cycle is simple. Everything starts with thought influenced by a belief, then there is an action that produces an outcome or consequence. This cycle repeats over and over every day in your life for every decision you make. The process may be at lightning speed if the decision is familiar to you or it may be slower if you need to take extra time at any one step. No matter what you do, beliefs are a catalyst after any thought about how you will take action.

The belief cycle is real. Every outcome you've ever created started as a thought (an emotionless idea) attached to a belief (a brain-shortcut for life). You would have then taken an action. As you move forward, know that this cycle continues to drive your choices. Know that the quality of any idea is always less important than the quality and strength of the belief behind it. Set your energy and intention on understanding, uncovering, improving, and transforming your beliefs. You will find yourself closer to what the crows said, "You have to believe you can fly before you can fly."

I can always tell if an individual's beliefs are working for them or blocking them from their next step. It's a clue you may not expect but is powerfully revealing about how your beliefs are influencing your resilience and actions. Your clothes including what you choose, why you wear them, and what symbolism you assign to them are all deeply influential to new self-belief conquering old self-doubt. It's a secret superpower if you can get it right.

Your Current Mindset is in Your Closet

Rediscovering yourself in a transition starts with exploring what you believe to be true about yourself and your life. This is not a new idea, but you may not realize that you can identify mindset tapes by looking at your dressing behavior. Remember, any action is a result of a thought mixed with a belief.

Let me introduce you to an idea that connects your resilience and confidence:

Every day you ask yourself, "What should I wear?" That's a thought. Whether you know it or not, it will be influenced by your current mindset (your blueprint of belief). Whoa, right?

I've watched countless women get dressed without knowing how reflective their dressing behavior is of their current mindset. In the midst of transition, you experience feelings of chaos, confusion, aimlessness, frustration, and, the biggest, self-doubt. Self-doubt rules the mindset blueprint that doesn't serve you in a transition and is the villain of confidence. It's the opposite of the sureness of self.

I've coached and mentored thousands of women in their image-confidence and when I see a woman unintentionally wear all black, I know she's in a mindset where she's feeling misaligned from shifted priorities and it's leading her to feel uncertain about her next actions for keeping herself safe, secure, and thriving. Her old beliefs are running her dressing behavior and it will affect her ability to show up with confidence for her job, career, business, parents, and relationships.

I remember the day this connection hit me over the head. I was in my client's closet doing the typical "stylist's closet cleanout" appointment sorting by color and function, but something different happened. I got to the section of her closet with sweaters. I pulled out one limpy, dimpy cardigan with no body-flattering shape whatsoever. I pulled out one, then I pulled out another, and then another and one more. By the end of my pull, I was holding twenty lifeless, shapeless cardigan sweaters—all in either black or grey.

I then asked her the question which would change how I would coach women forever, "What do all of these mean to you?"

My client answered sheepishly, sounding almost personally defeated and said, "When I don't know what to do, I put those on. I feel like I can fade away."

BOOM mind blown. Connection revealed.

It's exactly what she had been doing in her life. The reason she wanted to work with an image consultant was because she wanted to land a promotion at work. She knew that for the position, she would need to showcase more presence to go along with her substance and capability, but she had been wearing these sweaters almost every day through the interview and evaluation process.

Then I asked her the next question which solidified the existence of her mindset living in her closet. I asked, "What do you believe about yourself right now about putting yourself forward for the promotion?"

She couldn't look at me as she said, "I don't know why they'd pick me. I've never been chosen for something so big before."

DOUBLE BOOM mind blown. Connection solidified.

She didn't believe she deserved to have the new, big opportunity and couldn't see herself in the position, so made herself fade away—her mindset was being mirrored in the actions of her dressing behavior.

Needless to say, we fixed her right up as I began to develop a new way of thinking about why, and then how, to prepare my women for the day. Prepare your mindset with your dressing actions and that mindset will flow into the actions for the rest of your day.

A new credo emerged and runs my work to this day:

The intention of your dressing becomes the intention of your day.

Your current mindset is an active blueprint that is influencing every action you take today including how you chose to get dressed. Moving yourself through any transition with the aim of healing and celebrating the person you are becoming requires you to watch your thoughts for the beliefs that misalign with where you are going.

Remember, "You have to believe you can fly" suggests that you own a mindset that supports success—starting with a belief that a new possibility exists. In the movie, the crows made Dumbo hold a feather that was supposedly magic and would help him fly. It gave him hope that success was possible. You have a "magic feather" too that you may not realize, but unlike Dumbo who dropped his and lost his belief, you'll never lose this new way of preparing yourself for your day and life. It's a compass you can use to stay true to beliefs that serve you and, believe it or not, can shift how you present yourself to show up for your day with confidence.

REFLECTION AND JOURNAL WORK

TODAY: Take a deep dive into your greatest hurts and greatest joys. What were they?

What mindset beliefs helped you overcome the hurt or experience the joy?

TOMORROW: There are a number of clues in your closet that are signals of your current mindset and self-belief, and they are running your current behavior for both your dressing and your momentum toward success. Identify how you feel while getting dressed today.

"When I think about getting dressed, I feel ___."

"After I get dressed and ready, I feel ___."

5

DEFINE YOUR CONFIDENCE COMPASS

"Confidence is self-love in action." ~MCG.

It's human nature to want to "find yourself" and to look for it through a transition. After high school, a few of my friends said they were going to take a year off to "find themselves." Some went backpacking across Europe, others went tree-planting. I didn't know what they were looking for and wondered if they would know when they found it. The idea of finding yourself can feel overwhelming but I have a secret, you already have a compass. You simply need to define the points.

In 1981, my family moved from Baltimore, Maryland to Canada and to a small Ukrainian farming town in Southern Saskatchewan called Yorkton. There was a lot to adapt to. It was cold. There was a lot of snow in the first winter, and we were very different. My sister Nicole and I were the only visible minorities in our entire elementary school and my Dad was known as "The Black Dentist."

For some, the difference was all about the visual. Our skin was darker. For many it was something they had never seen before. Some reactions were overtly racist, with name-calling and prejudiced actions like following us around stores. Other reactions came from non-malicious ignorance. I remember a little boy at my Dad's dental office asking his mother legitimately if Dr. Charles was made of chocolate. I felt unsettled after first hearing the story, but then later understood his question came from harmless ignorance. This child had never been exposed to anyone with darker skin.

Growing up as the "only ones" in our town, we didn't have anyone else who looked like us. My parents, and my Dad in particular, made a point of helping Nicole and I understand and embrace what was more important than the fact that we were girls (and Black girls, at that). He used Ms. Whitney Houston to help us learn it.

Every now and then, my Dad came into our shared room, kneeled down between our two twin beds, propped up the cassette player, plunked in the Whitney Houston cassette tape and pressed play. Whitney's voice filled the room and he sang along. He sang every word in his very bad falsetto—even hitting the high notes. Nicole and I giggled. I don't remember how many times he did this serenade exercise, but it was enough because I still know every word and nuance of that Whitney song and feel every lyric as is if he is right here with me.

Each time he sang this song, the lesson he was trying to teach us became more and more clear. It doesn't matter what the outside world thinks of you. If you have love for yourself . . . a relationship with yourself, you will live on your own terms creating your own happiness. There is only one person who will love and cherish you always—that is yourself. The exercise in bad singing introduced us to the very important idea of self-love as being essential to happiness. He taught us "The Greatest Love of All."

I still listen to Whitney's song. (You might enjoy it too.) It's another part of my belief blueprint and I revisit it when I need a reminder of my foundation. I've used it as a mindset reset button more than a few times after major transitions. The biggest moments of redefinition from being the only visible minority in town, to the passing of my Dad, to the birth of my daughter, all forced me to sift through my beliefs to find what was true to me on the other side of the change.

Finding yourself is less about the search I've found and more about the release of the old, acceptance of what you're learning and love for what you will offer the world moving forward. It's learning to honor the qualities of your gifts and talents and living with meaning through your personal virtues and values. You don't have to backpack across Europe to find yourself, you only need to be willing to spend good quality time with yourself defining your Confidence Compass which holds all the answers for what will make you happy and fulfilled.

Defining Your Confidence Compass

The reason Whitney's song resonates so deeply is because it speaks about the things that make you— you. Everything that makes you unique has power and when used intentionally creates an expression of your life that is like a fingerprint—that no one can copy.

When I wrote my children's book, Angel In Your Heart, I expressed this collection of qualities as gifts, talents, virtues and values. These four parts of you are like guide points on a compass and as with any compass, well-defined guiding points help you make your decisions, keep your commitments, choose wisely, and live joyfully.

Gifts, talents, virtues, and values express what is deeply unique about your best qualities, and also help you paint a picture of how to develop what's inside you to make the truest expression of yourself to others with what you do. This magical collection of attributes defines your purpose, gives meaning to work, and boosts fulfillment when they all come together in your daily life. They are your guiding principles in use, action, and discipline.

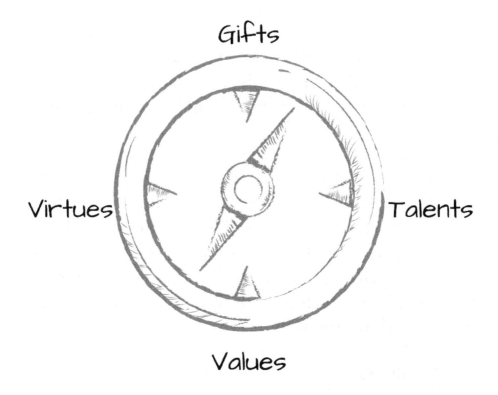

Gifts

Gifts are the most important part of the Confidence Compass. They are your true North and your guiding light. Gifts are qualities you have always owned. You may have heard people in your life say "you came out of the womb like that," or that you've always been this way. Gifts have been running in the background of your life since its beginning and for your entire life.

They have helped you create your greatest achievements and may have helped you earn success with what seemed like less effort than others. They have brought you joy when you were committed to using them, and when you forget about them, you find yourself sad, lost, aimless, or even depressed.

Gifts are divine. They are part of your unique spark. No one can own your collection of gifts and wield them like you do—once you know them. They are a unique combination to be discovered, celebrated, and treasured when they are used with intention. Over time, gifts become talents.

Examples: *Friendly, Trustworthy, Humorous, Open, Caring, Creative, Patient, Thoughtful*

Talents
Talents are gifts in action. They are qualities you develop as you do life exercising your gifts. They are not what you do. They are not your job title or even your job description. They are the superpowers you

own that make you excellent at a job you choose or amazing at your position. Talents are transferable to anything you do.

That's what makes them a superpower and because they come as a result of your own combination of gifts, how you use your talents also cannot be copied. Talents are powerful parts of you, but they require nurturing to turn them from something that you can do into a power that impacts others.

Talents require an investment of time, effort, and resources to develop. They aren't like gifts that you just have and that by default are what you can do at any moment. Talents will get better over time. When you continue to use, grow, practice and hone them with the discipline of personal growth, you are investing in your future. Making the investment in your talents pays off because they do something very important.

Talents solve problems for yourself and for others. Used purposefully, talents will help you define a career, choose a vocation, rule out a job, help you start a business that no one has ever thought of before, or maybe they'll help you move up in an organization where you can find more fulfillment because you can make more of an impact on others.

Examples: *Deciding, Teaching, Problem Solving, Comforting, Connecting, Strategizing, Leading, Unifying, Organizing, Analyzing, Building, Designing*

Values

Values are the goal of living a good life. They are your definition of your life. They are aspirational railroad tracks about how we see life and how we want to experience life. Living with clearly defined values, you will choose your partner, your career path, and even the company you work for using them as a guide. When things align with our values, they will seem to fit and will feel like a match in our lives.

Examples: *Security, Excellence, Community, Confidence, Growth, Love, Joy, Service, Peace, Freedom, Independence, Integrity, Truth, Justice, Unity*

Virtues

Virtues are your values in action. It's easy to confuse the two since the meanings are often used interchangeably, but virtues are the characteristics that you exercise on a consistent basis that create a life lived according to values. Virtues are the train engine. While values are the train tracks, virtues create the power and the momentum to keep you on track for a life you love.

Examples: *Discipline, Honesty, Fairness, Strength, Tolerance, Respect, Loyalty, Helpfulness, Faithfulness, Openness, Kindness, Trust, Purposefulness, Cooperation*

Taking the time to uncover your gifts, talents, virtues, and values is the very first essential step to rediscovering new self-love. When you identify your gifts, talents, virtues, and values, you begin to see yourself as important and then you start to realize that this important person has an important contribution to make—self-love starts to blossom.

Everyone has a Confidence Compass, no matter your vocation, role, status or stature, though it can be easy to lose it as life shifts. One of my dear clients found new power in defining her Compass and it changed everything.

Delaina is a teacher but more than that she is a natural educator, but like so many educators, through the years of dealing with "the system" while also trying to navigate her own dips in confidence from motherhood and marriage shifts, Delaina was tired. In her words, "I was dim."

The first day we met one-on-one, I was looking to hire her as my virtual assistant. I had called her a few days earlier and left a message to call me back so we could book this appointment. She later told me she didn't have the confidence to call me right away. She left my message on her voicemail for two days before she finally got the courage to return my call.

We met at an ordinary local coffee shop and we talked about what I needed. I knew right away she had the talent—organized, thorough, responsive, and experienced—but I could also see and feel that Delaina, herself, didn't believe in what I could see. She pulled her blouse and shifted in her chair. Her body language seemed to say, "I don't belong in this seat in front of this woman." Her self-doubt from life's challenges had clouded her view from seeing her value and taking her seat at my coffee shop table; so much so, that she almost sabotaged her opportunity to have me as a client by not calling me back.

At the end of our coffee, while nervously tapping her pen on her notebook, she bit her lip and with a trickle of courage, she said, "Michele, can I participate in your program?" Her eyes met mine as soon as the words came out and seemed to soften with surprise mixed with relief that she had actually gotten the words out. Her chin lifted with a swell of resolve and as if to convince herself she said, "If I'm going to work for an image consultant, I better look like I've worked with an image consultant." I smiled back warmly as if I knew a juicy secret, because what I knew before she could ever know was that she was about to get herself back—not her style—but herself.

With me, Delaina rediscovered her gifts and talents, which sparked a new self-worth to grow her VA business at a speed that left her in awe. New clients came effortlessly. With her refreshed clarity of her confidence compass and my mentorship to direct her life by it, mixed with the process I taught her to present her intentions and be seen for it, in the years to come, Delaina would stand up in her teaching career when she saw injustice, would use her voice to make social change at her school, and would start a new business as a certified confidence coach for kids, helping to support their resilience skills. Delaina would gain the notice and admiration of her col-leagues for her unwavering commitment to "the kids" and she would be offered leadership positions that she knew without question she deserved. Beyond that, Delaina used her deep understanding of her gifts, talents, virtues, and values to redesign her family life, saving her marriage, deepening her relationship with her kids and repairing her connec-tion with her mother.

That "dim" was long gone and replaced with a life she loved.

Delaina later said to me, "Michele, thank you is never going to be enough. I did the work, but you lit me up."

A confidence compass is a guide. It's a tool to love yourself and your life authentically. It's a source of comfort and power and when defined and used with intention sets you free.

REFLECTION AND JOURNAL WORK

TODAY: Spend time with your gifts and talents. Think back to the times of your greatest hurts and grandest joys. What gifts have you always owned that helped you resolve these changes? What talents helped you create new outcomes that made you happier, more fulfilled, and more satisfied?

Examples of GIFTS: Friendly, Trustworthy, Humorous, Open, Caring, Creative, Patient, Thoughtful

Add Your Own Ideas:

Examples of TALENTS: Deciding, Teaching, Problem Solving, Comforting, Connecting, Strategizing, Leading, Unifying, Organizing, Analyzing, Building, Designing

Add Your Own Ideas:

TOMORROW: Spend time with values and virtues. What are the common threads in your life experiences that reveal what is most important about living your life. What values are non-negotiable and must be present in all of your decisions? What virtues do you hold yourself responsible for displaying in your actions?

Examples of VALUES: Security, Excellence, Community, Confidence, Growth, Love, Joy, Service, Peace , Freedom, Independence, Integrity, Truth, Justice, Unity

Add Your Own Ideas:

Examples of VIRTUES: Discipline, Honesty, Fairness, Strength, Tolerance, Respect, Loyalty Helpfulness, Faithfulness, Openness, Kindness, Trust, Purposefulness, Cooperation

Add Your Own Ideas:

THE NEXT DAY: Draw your personal Confidence Compass from which you set your course to make all forward-moving decisions and choices.

Section II

ENERGIZE

6

DISCOVER YOUR WHISPERED LESSONS

"Curiosity is the seed of purpose." ~MCG.

My mom, as my model for resilience, taught me how to see life as a lesson-filled journey designed for me to grow. She modeled how to trust your intuition without question and use it to find new ways to do what you think you can't. My mom was the first one to teach me to find lessons of life from quiet contemplation. In those moments, is where you can hear the clues for new meaning and purpose. They come as quiet as a whisper.

My mom had a kitchen office where the family calendar lived to write in events and activities. There were pens, and the phone, and places to hang up phone messages. There was also a little nook inside one of the shelves where she kept a few inspirational quotes tacked to a pinboard—mostly by Maya Angelou, but there were some others tossed in:

"When people show you who they are ———— believe them." M/A Angela

"You did then what you knew how to do, when you knew better; you did better." Mya Angelo

"You don't have to see the whole staircase just take the first step." Dr MARTIN LUther KINg

"Clutter is Postponed Decisions."

Sorting Rules:
- Friends
- Aquaintanaes
- Strangers
- First Name

Just before I left to travel over 3,000 kilometers across the country to university, she unpinned a slip of paper with faded words that looked like it had been photocopied many times. On it was this message:

```
        Keep watch, listen and learn.
            When God wants us to
               Learn a lesson
      He will send use clues in the form of
                 some kind of
       Communication. It will appear as a:

              1.    WHISPER
              2.    MESSAGE
              3.    PROBLEM
              4.    DIASTER
```

My mom's typical presence is one that commands the room. With broad shoulders and a proud chest, she holds space as a protector of those she loves—just as a left-tackle would protect a quarterback's blindside. In this moment though, her shoulders fell as protective duty softened to nurturing care and concern. The shift surprised me and I knew I needed to listen to what was coming next.

With the flick of her wrist she handed me the slip of paper and said, "This is important, you'll need it." She started to share in this rarely revealed softness that every challenge in life teaches you a lesson about how to grow stronger, keep yourself safe, and bounce back. The lesson will repeat itself until you learn it.

I asked, "How will I know something is supposed to be a lesson?"

"Everything is," she said without hesitation, "There's no good or bad things that happen to you, only lessons for you to learn."

She went on to explain how to recognize a lesson, referencing the faded slip of paper:

- The lesson will start as a whisper. It will quietly offer you small clues to something that doesn't serve you, is misaligned, or not right for you. The lesson may feel like an annoyance or an itchy intuition that "something isn't right." The lesson will wait for your conviction and action to resolve it. If none, it will return to you as a message.
- The lesson as a message will be something that causes inconvenience or that becomes a bigger obstacle you need to "jump over." The lesson will wait for your conviction and action, if none, it will return to you as a problem.
- A problem will cost you something—time,

money, effort, or a piece of yourself. This is the last chance to catch the lesson before it begins to spiral. The lesson will wait for your conviction and action, if none, it will return to you as a disaster.

- A disaster causes a total dismantling of what you thought to be true. It leaves you feeling disoriented, in chaos, aimless, drained, and clouded from seeing what is next. It's your lowest point but is still an opportunity to grow and emerge better than before.

With a glint in her eye like she knew a secret she was only sharing with me, my Mom advised me to "see the lesson coming at a whisper." To make decisions, choices, and changes that would keep the lesson from progressing. She offered hope too, sharing that once you've learned the right lesson, a blessing is right behind it. Watch for those too.

When this happens; take heed and do what the message tells you before you have a disaster . Cause if you don't listen and learn the lesson,God will give you the lesson again and again until you learn it.
So learn the lesson with a **Whisper**.

Going off to college at 18, I couldn't fully appreciate what my Mom meant by "lessons" nor could I fully grasp what a whisper, message, problem, or disaster could, or would, look like in my life. I do remember early on though thinking about and questioning, what about tragedies or unexpected devastations happening? Isn't that a disaster? What can a person do when something seems so out of control? Is it life scolding or punishing someone for something when that happens?

It wasn't until I lost my Dad at twenty-four years old that I realized that's not how it works. Many would think this life event would be a disaster. In fact, I came to see it through the filter of the life lessons I will talk about in a minute. His passing was actually a lesson of self-worth and courage for me.

Terrible things happen. Things that make you hurt will happen, but how you see it and the lesson you choose to learn for yourself will change the meaning for you. The whispering lessons of life are never about anything outside yourself. They are never about the event that happened to you, they are about how you find meaning in what has happened to you. Meaning from the transition is what turns hurt, loss, or sadness into new clarity, gratitude, and healing. The event becomes an opportunity to see the lesson that helps you grow. It took a little more than a decade for me to distill and define "the lessons" life was trying to teach me with all of its whispering, and it didn't come easily.

Defining The Lessons
SUCCESS = WINNING

Growing up, I liked to win. I wasn't into athletics. I was into academics and grades. Recognition for my effort became my motivation. The quest worked for me for a long time. I won awards in school, stepped into leadership positions, started an entrepreneur's association at my university, became chairperson of community boards, gave time, gave energy, gave presence to cause after cause. I received recognition, validation, proof that I was "good enough" and that nothing could hold me back if I just kept winning.

By twenty-five, I was a seasoned entrepreneur, a respected business community figure in my town. I was the president of the Chamber of Commerce, in the top 1% of a direct sales company, had been recognized as the #5 top team-builder in the country, had earned diamonds and jewels, and was making great money. I was winning on all accounts.

Then it all changed when my daughter B was born.

SUCCESS = NOT LOSING

I had built my business in such a way that I was able to enjoy my full commission check with no "dip" in income while on maternity leave—WIN! I was taking the time I needed to be with B to get her on a schedule and routine. She was even sleeping through the night at six weeks old—WIN!

I should have been happy to hang out for a year or more of maternity leave and enjoy the experience. But no. I was back to working in five months. Success now was about "not losing" things that were important to me: momentum, what I had established, what I had built, or my sense of worth.

I spent the next few years trying not to lose my need for recognition that I was "good enough" in the only way it made sense to me—my work. I changed jobs to try to win. I trained for and ran a half-marathon (even though since then, I've realized I don't really like running), I did it to feel "a win," but something was missing.

In 2010, it all crashed. The quest to want to "win" in a way that would make me feel good, like myself—valuable and recognized, wasn't working. Even though all these wins stacked in my past and in my favor, I fell into a depression. I call it the "sad times." It's hard to describe but I can liken the feeling to being in fog. You feel disoriented, can't see in front of you, and feel yourself losing hope. That loss of hope shows up in beliefs and behavior.

Looking back, I remember nights of having too much wine watching TV feeling numb and lost. It scared me but I didn't know what to do with the feeling. These feelings peaked one day as I cried uncontrollably to my mentor at the time. He calmly slid a card with the number of a counselor across his desk and said, "Michele, I think this is what you need right now."

On the call with the counselor, I told her about the experience of never being able to watch A&E's Intervention where families confront their drug or alcohol addicted family members in an effort to offer them help and hope. I told her that in the past, it would make me physically nauseous to watch the addict shoot their drug of choice into their body. I used to avoid watching or change the channel. This day on the call with the councillor, I admitted to her that not only was I able to watch, but I could relate. I could understand why they wanted to numb and disappear. Saying it to her scared me.

The counselor, in a most compassionate tone, told me that I was right to be scared. I was one step away from being that person on the show. I clearly remember her telling me, "Michele, you are on the brink."

From that day on, I knew I had to change. I was not prepared to lose the goodness of my life to anything. The counselor told me to pay close attention to myself. I started and began to recover. I started by redefining what it meant to "win" in my life and to ask "what am I supposed to be learning about myself?" The Whispered Lessons are the answers. There are four of them:

- Self-Worth
- Courage

- Compassion
- Discipline

I could see that each of these lessons played a role in why I had attached my value to achievement and why it was no longer working to make myself happy—producing heavy sadness. I immediately saw these lessons had repeated themselves in my life anytime it felt "hard." I also realized that the times I put conviction and focus on them and took action with them; those were the times I had my most satisfying triumphs, recoveries, and successes. These lessons are calling to you each time you have a dip in confidence; those times in a transition where your life's priorities need to be realigned.

The Whispered Lessons take the form of a pyramid. Each level on the pyramid is a lesson for – your soul. For any area of your life's priorities, you start learning the lesson at the base and work your way up. As you do, you grow.

The pyramid is a metaphor of how each lesson layers onto the next. The biggest, most important to resolve, is on the bottom and the most powerfully transforming on the inside, and out is on the top.

Discipline

Compassion

Courage

Self-Worth

Self-Worth

Your capacity to know your value and to honor your uniqueness. It's having clarity around your purpose and finding meaning in the contribution you make in any area of your life. It's internal. It requires contemplation and a relationship with yourself that is cherished and nurtured. When you have self-worth you will have,

Courage

Your ability to summon bravery in the face of fear and to know that you can, and will, keep yourself safe no matter what. It's trusting yourself first after listening intently to what you need to be happy and fulfilled. When you have solid inside courage you will share it with yourself and others through,

Compassion

Your ability to care for and forgive yourself first and then others. It's seeing yourself as needing love and concern and that is mirrored in how you give it to others. Compassion is where the inside lesson begins to move outside yourself.

Discipline

Your ability to do what you know needs to be done for the greater good whether you feel like it at the moment or not. It shows up as the decisions and choices you make that serve the other three. It's the doing after the feeling and when aligned with your self-worth and your beliefs is where personal growth happens and personal power—confidence—blossoms.

In any area of your life, you'll be experiencing a lesson somewhere on the pyramid. Not all areas carry the same lesson. For instance, it's possible to have worked through the self-worth lesson that helps you understand that you deserve health, you may be able to have the courage to start a new exercise program after asking for help and you may be practicing self-compassion by creating a routine. You may then be currently working on the discipline to follow through. And though you may be working on Discipline in your health, you may find that you are sitting at a self-worth lesson in your career.

Almost all of my clients begin their work with me thinking they are stuck because they can't stay motivated to do the disciplined tasks that get them the success they want. Very early in my process, they learn it's not the discipline. I help them rewrite their self-worth at warp speed which opens up access to the other lessons for themselves and the people around them. As they move up the pyramid, they find more energy to work the "discipline."

Harpreet is a go-getter, professional and award-winning realtor. When we met, she was a new mom to her daughter and was feeling stuck in the mommy-fog wondering if she could get back her high-achieving definition of herself and also grieving the passing of her brother. She was stuck; her vibrant personality was clouded by her grief. She was at the bottom of the pyramid and she was making choices that were keeping her worth invisible, presenting herself every day in all black everything—black car, black clothes. Harpreet was an extrovert lingering in the background of her life, but she knew she wanted more.

She leaned over my table at our first meeting and with stiff resolve in her voice and a spark of fire in her eye she said, "I've gotta snap outta this. I want more business and I have to be able to put myself out there to do it. That's why you're my new Image Consultant." We went to work in my process.

She used that refreshed self-worth in her image to climb the Whispered Lessons pyramid resolving her new purpose after grief and aligning her choices in business for her family balance. The discipline she needed followed swiftly and she not only began to flourish again but found a renewed love of her twenty plus year career. She finished the self-worth lesson with the help of my process and then built on its momentum for a rush of confidence that changed how she created success in her life.

Because confidence comes from finishing, when you "finish" a lesson—whether it's a whisper, message, problem, or disaster—by making choices that align with your values, outcome, purpose, and intentions, you will feel a rush of confidence that feeds your next step. For any challenge or tough times, if you can distill which place you are standing in the lesson and, at what kind of "whisper" it is, after quiet contemplation, you will see exactly what to learn from it which gives you clarity about your actions to overcome all in an attempt for it not to repeat—a personal growth WIN!

When I started to use this perspective and match it with my Confidence Compass, it fed my renewal faster than ever and set me up for the next step of redefining purpose. Seeing life's lessons in this way will help you to do the following:

- Connect with your inner voice and intuition.
- Make more aligned decisions, faster.
- Detach yourself from the opinions of others.
- Release the need to justify your choices.

I did add one step to my mom's list that created a powerful intention: speak the lesson out loud. Name, call out, or write down the lesson you're learning. This activates a new spark of belief in your mindset and, by now, you know that is a powerful activator for making change. It makes each action you take—from self-worth, to courage, to compassion, to discipline—more impactful.

REFLECTION & JOURNAL WORK

TODAY: Where have you learned your biggest lessons? At a whisper, message, problem, or disaster? Describe in detail.

TOMORROW: Explore a recent transition; what lesson are you challenged to learn?

For that priority area of your life, try asking yourself the following questions:

What about my self-worth do I need to know here?

What is it that I need to be brave to do? What am I avoiding?

Am I caring toward myself in this lesson or am I putting others over myself? If I'm feeling cared for, in what way do I need to turn that care and concern outward to others? How am I acting with the discipline to carry this out?

Activate the lesson you are learning. Call it out. Ask the question: "What am I learning here?" Speak it out loud with new intention.

THE NEXT DAY: Free write, mediate, or express in any way you choose about how your most significant Whispered Lessons have woven into past choices and behaviors. Can you see a connection where you were stifled and where you excelled?

7

OWN YOUR MEANINGFUL OUTCOME

"Purpose powers your confidence." ~MCG.

Purpose is a word with a BIG calling.

Everywhere you look, you're asked to define it, find it, and live it. We all want to feel important, valued, and that our contribution of our time on the planet is meaningful, so knowing your purpose and exercising it can feel like a heavy responsibility. Let me ease your longing for "the search" for your purpose by letting you in on a little secret: you already have it.

It's just below the surface already connected to your Confidence Compass and the potential result of committing to learn your Whispered Lessons. Living with purpose is the ultimate expression of your sureness of self—your confidence, your bounce-backability—your resilience. Your purpose is the bridge between the work you do on the inside for yourself and what you do for others. I call your purpose your life's Meaningful Outcome.

Your Meaningful Outcome is something that produces results for yourself and others. It has very specific criteria and it's magical if it does any, and ideally all of these things. A Meaningful Outcome does the following:

- Creates happiness
- Produces a lasting transformation
- Fosters confidence
- Helps others find joy

The longer you stay in alignment with your Compass, you determine a clear definition and living expression of your Meaningful Outcome. Then, the longer you deliver that outcome repeatedly over time, the wider, deeper, and more satisfying impact you make—and the bigger and bolder joy you will feel.

You don't need to be a blockbuster celebrity with 110 million followers on social media to make a wide and deep impact. You simply need a Meaningful Outcome that you practice consistently over time. Not only does it become a focused direction for your life, it becomes how people know and remember you—it leaves a legacy.

Leaving Your Legacy

You may find yourself concerned with leaving a legacy with your life. Let me ease that worry too. A Meaningful Outcome offered and exercised over and over and over again with consistency and intention becomes a legacy. A legacy is for what, and how, you will be remembered by those you've impacted and changed. The idea of legacy doesn't just lie with celebrities. When you live through your Meaningful Outcome, you will have a number of people, big or small, you help be better. That's where legacy is created—it lives in those we change.

Think of people you have in your life you look up to—even those you've never met or watch from afar. What legacy are they leaving, or have they left? If you sit in reflection long enough, you'll see that anyone you admire has a roster of gifts, talents, values, and virtues you can name, and that you can see have been used to make an impression on your life. THAT is legacy. Legacy leavers can be anyone from a parent to your sport team coach to your grade seven English teacher.

Legacy Leaver: The Painless Dentist

My dad, Dr. Gerald Sonson Charles Jr., was a dentist by job title, but his values and commitment to his Meaningful Outcome for his patients made him so much more. He was a purveyor of confidence. He used to say "Smile and the whole world smiles with you." He made it his purpose to help people have the confidence to smile. From his values he gave them excellence in service, a pleasant experience from his charisma and painless, innovative dentistry from cultivating his talent as a mechanical engineer. To this day, decades after his passing, and practicing dentistry, his patients remember what he gave them.

These are what created his legacy of delivering lasting transformations in health while being an example in his field. Do you see how all the parts of gift, talent, virtues, and values fit? This is how impact, legacy, and a life fully lived is built. You can do it too at any time in your life. You can define your Meaningful Outcome based on exactly who you are at the moment even after a transition.

Legacy Leaver: The Belief Teacher

Mrs. Jenson, whom I can now confidently call Fern because of how close we've grown together, was my grade seven English teacher. She was also my first confidence mentor outside my family. Fern leaves a legacy as someone who breathes belief into others. For as long as I've known her, this is what she has done.

She used her Confidence Compass to inspire students like me and her fellow teachers. She has a caring and supportive approach that she uses to share her Meaningful Outcome of teaching those around her to express themselves with their full potential. These are her gifts and talents. She did it for me in her English class with a commitment to helping her students master the grammar that would help us put words to paper and express ourselves. She also did it with kind words on notecards in the time I spent with her in the direct sales company where she was my recruiter and mentor. Card after card, word after word in beautiful cursive came to me with every achievement or milestone mirroring back what she saw in me. She may not have known it at the time but what she wrote in her "belief notes" reflected back to me my most valuable gifts and talents and quietly reinforced my self-belief, helping me take more and more action, and produce more and more results.

Fern has a legacy whether she knows it or not, and like many humble, yet dedicated, legacy-builders, they do it in a way that seems quiet—away from the flashing lights of celebrity and influence—but in their small circles, in quiet moments, and with personal touches. These kinds of legacy builders make the most lasting heart-to-heart impact. They change the world.

Uncovering Your Meaningful Outcome

Getting to the expression of your own Meaningful Outcome requires you to focus wholeheartedly on the same reflection practices that helped you discover your Confidence Compass. Then you will need to go a step further and see the common threads between who you are and what you do to create change in others with the criteria of a Meaningful Outcome.

To find it, scan your life for the feelings of emptiness or dissatisfaction. Think back to the times in your life that felt totally misaligned, where you experienced overwhelm or burnout. In those times, you were missing a connection to your Meaningful Outcome. It was just below the surface begging to be found using your Confidence Compass. There is a connection. The exciting part of uncovering this part of yourself is it sets the stage for defining what success looks like beyond the narrow definition of "winning and losing," but where ultimate freedom and fulfillment lie.

REFLECTION AND JOURNAL WORK

TODAY: Think of a time you were most fulfilled, happy, and satisfied. How were you using your Confidence Compass?

What Meaningful Outcome were you giving others?

TOMORROW: Think of a time you were stressed or burnt out. How were you not expressing your Meaningful Outcome?

What parts of your Confidence Compass were not being honored by your choices?

THE NEXT DAY: Write a phrase or statement of your Meaningful Outcome that serves yourself and others. Measure it against your experiences of being happy and not. Now, think of how you can apply this definition to the priorities that need your attention.

How can you weave them together for more joy and results?

8

CREATE A PERSONAL DEFINITION OF SUCCESS

"Clarity creates freedom." ~MCG.

Versions of "success" have been defined by media, social media, and everything outside ourselves, but what is your definition? How would you define it? How would you express it? Is it money? Position? Status or lifestyle? I think, academically, you know that there is so much more to the Definition of Success than what you materialize in the outside world and that personal meaning is the road to fulfillment and happiness, but how do you actually define it?

When I was a sales manager for a direct sales company, it was my job to introduce women to the business opportunity. During my business marketing interview, I made a point of asking women what their personal Definition of Success was to start their businesses. Many of them couldn't tell me. They didn't know what I meant. They would ask," You mean how much money do I want to make?"

"No," I would say, "What does it mean for you to be successful? Is it money or something else?"

They would look at me like I had three heads. What else was there? It was during that time that I realized we're all presented with a very narrow scope of how to express our own personal definitions of success. I also found that if I could help them pinpoint it and articulate it, it gave them more motivation to do anything outside their comfort zone for personal and business growth.

Learning to define success and then live to it and through your Meaningful Outcome makes magic in your life. I've seen it in my own life and countless times in my client's lives. Even a beginner's understanding will serve to give you awareness when someone asks, "What does it mean to you to be successful?"

Your Definition of Success will be as personal as your fingerprint. I read once that "The purpose of your purpose is to help others find theirs." I agree. Your Definition of Success is what you receive back—the fruit of your labour—from exercising your Meaning Outcome.

Definitions of Success shift and change over time as transition happens, but you always have one that's leading and one that supports it. When you work for them, with what you do, happiness and satisfaction blossoms.

There are no more-noble than others definitions of success. They are all equal and your personal combination will be unique to your Confidence Compass and Meaningful Outcome.

The Definitions of Success
There are six definitions of success. You will have a dominant one and a secondary one at any point in

your life. They are the reasons you do something, or the reason you put motivation behind anything. The acronym that will help you remember the definitions is:

MRS E. FAB

Money

Recognition

Self-Esteem

Example To Others

Friends

Advancement

Be Your Own Boss

Money

Money is not the root of all evil. Money represents choices—especially for women. It means having the ability to say "yes" when you want to, "no" when you need to, it gets you out of certain situations, and can put you in other opportunities. Money is a tool for making new choices.

Having money as a Definition of Success will reflect what you value—maybe education or adventure. You may want to help your kids get a higher education. That requires money. You may dream to own a lake home to create family memories. That requires money. Money gets a bad rep. Think of it as a tool. To have it as a definition simply means you want more choices.

Recognition

Recognition is being acknowledged for your contribution. Admitting you like recognition is not being boastful or attention-seeking; it simply means that you want others to understand that the difference you make is important. Being recognized may complement the way you want to make an impact by making you more visible to those who you can help or to those you can partner with to help you create. Recognition is not about being showy—it's about being seen so you are in a position to do more for more.

Self-Esteem

Sometimes our motivation is to heal ourselves. Healing your self-esteem (how you think about and value yourself) helps create the self-love needed to build confidence in your abilities. Taking actions that prioritize personal discovery, growth, and dismantling of old beliefs that hold us back clear space in our mind and hearts to offer more to others. This can be becoming a better parent, a better community leader, or even a better partner.

Example to Others

Being an example to others is a desire to step into a leadership role. Helping others can be intensely fulfilling and self-motivating. Live and model your values and you will inspire others to do the same—building your family, teams, organizations, and communities.

No matter who follows you, you see the importance of living a life of example, so others have a positive role model to emulate. Your actions with this Definition of Success are deliberate and consistent, knowing that you may not see the impact of your example immediately but that they eventually will become part of those you inspire.

Friends and Supportive Relationships

We all crave and need connection with people who "get us." As you go through life, there is a reason and a season for any relationship you will have. Some seasons last decades, some years, some months, and some minutes. The kinds of relationships you need at a particular time in your life will either move you forward, keep you stagnant, or pull you backward.

Choosing friends and relationships as a Definition of Success means you are committed to adding and maintaining relationships that support the impact you want to make. It may be with your partner/spouse, it may be prioritizing certain types of collaborations knowing they support your own personal growth that moves you to the next level of success.

Advancement

The desire to achieve can have a negative connotation or be grouped with workaholics or wanting to win at all costs. Taken purely on its own, achievement and advancement is much like recognition. When it is paired with purpose, it becomes a way to reach more and create a larger and deeper impact. Moving up may mean reaching and impacting more people with your purpose.

Advancement may put you in more influential circles that give you the stage to bring your new ideas to life. Having advancement as a Definition of Success is not about vanity, it's about claiming a position of leadership intentionally.

Be Your Own Boss

Being your own "boss" simply means being in charge of your own agenda. It may mean flexibility in how you work whether you work for yourself or you're an ambitious, independent go-getter inside an organization. It means you value individuality and the ability to layer your perspective over the work you do—to be able to speak in your voice with freedom. When this is a Definition of Success, autonomy is important, allowing you to tailor your purpose for the stage of life or your audience's needs.

There was a short year where I worked in the finance department of a car dealership. I had just stepped out of full-time entrepreneurship after ten years of being the leader of a sales team in a direct sales company. I thought I wanted something different but that would still use my sales expertise and people skills. The job was great! I excelled with my coworkers and customers. The people were great! We laughed a lot and it felt like family most times.

What wasn't great was the lifestyle. I remember the exact moment I was forced to work my own process. The dealership was holding an off-site indoor sale for ten days. These sales were always a stint of long hours and high stress. It wasn't unusual to work more than twelve-hour days. Some wouldn't mind having time with fun coworkers and ordering out for Chinese food, but I did. I minded very much. I had an eighteen-month-old daughter at home.

It was always part of my Definition of Success to be flexible enough in my work that I could tend to my family at any time I needed to without needing anyone's approval. It's why I've been such a disciplined entrepreneur and had been for the ten years before this incident.

One night at the indoor sale, I was "working a deal" with the salesperson and the customer and I received a call from my husband, Chris. The first thing he said freaked me right out, "I don't want you to worry, she's fine."

What! Like are you kidding me? You can't ever tell a mother, "Don't worry, she's fine." And not have the worry shoot from zero to a thousand.

My eyes got wide, my breathing quickened as I tried to remain composed with my job on one end of the phone and my family on the other. I was literally caught in the middle.

Chris explained that B had tripped on the way to her bath and fell and hit her mouth on the edge of the tub. Her front tooth was chipped.

WHAT! This might sound minor to you, but for me, the daughter of a dentist, and a victim of a trip and fall accident with my sister that made my front tooth turn black—I was panicked already running through how I was going to call my dentist friend to do emergency surgery.

I was sling-shotted out of panic and into guilt when I looked up and saw the salesperson with his customer at my office door. I had a deal on my desk.

Right here. This was the turning point—the moment the game changed.

I calmed down enough to tell Chris I would figure something out and hung up the phone. Then I asked the customer to wait in my office as I went to find the sales manager. I explained the emergency. I explained that I had a deal and though he was understanding enough to be ok with me going home to see how B was doing, it was me who felt like I had done the wrong thing by leaving and so I promised him I'd be back in forty-five minutes.

Twenty of those minutes was spent driving there and back which means I only had twenty-five minutes to get through the door, hear the story again, to see if the tooth needed to be put in milk to save, to hug my kid, to ask about if she had taken some Tylenol, to call my dentist friend, Sonia, and get her ready if she needed to see her right away. All was fine. It was just a chip on a baby tooth which means it would eventually fall out and Sonia said she could file it down so it wouldn't be too sharp—that could happen over the coming days. All was fine, but I was not.

As I used the remainder of my forty-five minutes driving back to the indoor sale, I decided. Never again would I make that kind of choice. Never again would I feel bad about being torn. I saw my Definition of Success clear as day—be my own boss. I knew that eventually I would go back to entrepreneurship. From then I began to plan my escape. I knew that whatever I did in the meantime until I could get the kind of flexibility that was important to me, I would need to demand a flexible schedule. That was number one above Money, above Advancement, above all else.

You will have an experience or two that will be a clue to your ideal Definition of Success. Spend time uncovering it. When you know it, you will make choices that feel exactly right, will help you see your lessons, will make resilience stronger, and will spark new confidence to trust yourself at any moment.

Definitions of Success do change over time but if you are always in tune with your transitions, you'll be able to feel when it's time to pivot with them. None are more important, or more worthy, than the other, they only exist with the meaning you place on them for the happiness you wish to create.

The most powerful way to use your chosen Definition of Success is as a filter and scorecard for your Meaningful Outcome. When you consistently make decisions and take actions that use your Confidence Compass and serve your Meaningful Outcome, your Definition of Success will materialize, and you start to feel very good about yourself and what you're doing. If you don't feel very good, it's because one of these three pillars of your confidence are misaligned with another.

Immediately commit to rediscovery. Uncover a recent change, see your transition, understand which priorities have become misaligned from your Compass, reconnect your purpose and check-in with your Definition of Success. This is a magical practice and fast-track to new confidence from resilience.

REFLECTION AND JOURNAL WORK

TODAY: Think of a time when you didn't feel very good about yourself, about what you were doing or both. Which Definition of Success were you missing that would have fulfilled you?

TOMORROW: Think of a time you felt powerful, in control, and fulfilled. Which Definition of Success were you getting in abundance?

THE NEXT DAY: Consider your current situation (and possibly your recent transition). Which Definition of Success are you trying to achieve?

In what way are you working toward alignment of your Confidence Compass, your Meaningful Outcome and your Definition of Success?

*Bonus Reflection: How will you know when you've achieved your alignment? What will it look like?

9

SEE YOURSELF DIFFERENTLY

———————

"See yourself as who you are becoming." ~MCG.

Discovering what you're learning about yourself through transition, giving meaning to each step, and recognizing your importance produces a kind of motivation that is self-propelling. Over the years, I've been asked, "Michele, how do you keep yourself motivated?" Each time, I must make a face that says, "It's not what you think."

Motivation doesn't just show up. It doesn't come from a post you read on social media. It doesn't even come from pushing yourself or working hard. Motivation comes from connection and alignment. It comes from preparing yourself to be yourself and then showing up in that truth time after time.

Have you ever noticed that when you've decided something is for you or that you're into something that motivation is never a problem? It seems to be there even if for other people it might be hard? Seeing yourself as part of whatever you've decided is for you, shifts you toward becoming it. You change into it.

Here's an example. I love salsa dancing. Now. But when I was learning how in my second year of university, I didn't like it the first few times I went to lessons. I couldn't get the rhythm which annoyed me because I was a band geek and the daughter of a St. Lucian who loved to dance. Why the heck couldn't I pick this up already?

I was frustrated but for some reason I couldn't put it down. I didn't quit going to class. I just kept going and being frustrated. Had I not seen the part of salsa that represented me, I would have quit after the first class. It took about three classes to know why it WAS for me, what it touched in me, and what kept me coming back again and again to learn the steps even though it was frustrating the heck out of me. I could see myself becoming a salsa dancer. Here's why:

Salsa music is complex, and I love it. There's no beat-holding instrument guiding you where to step to be in rhythm. The beat is made up of all the instruments playing to their own rhythms. Once I figured out that I could step on the beat of the conga, shimmy to the song of the trumpet, footwork to the cowbell, I loved the freedom I had to express myself. Not coincidentally, freedom of expression is one of my most important values. That love of freedom of expression helped me find myself in the music and kept me motivated to master the dance. Once I got it, I was hooked. Since then, put on a song, and I'll dance it!

You too can create this kind of self-propelling motivation for anything you want to achieve and, guess what, it can start the moment you arrive at your mirror each day.

Looking in the mirror isn't the same thing as seeing yourself in the mirror. To look is to observe, to notice features, to use the mirror as a tool for utility. You may use it to style your hair, to brush on some mascara, to apply lipstick, but what you see is different than just a reflection. When you see yourself through the mirror, you can summon confidence and power.

The mirror might be a part-time lover and a fuller time enemy for you. Maybe it's been the thing to point out the insecurities and imperfections through your life; adolescent breakouts to young adult body changes. Mirrors hold such positions of judgement for most of us, but it's possible to reframe its influence on your self-belief.

You are not what you look at in the mirror. You are what you see. When you develop a new relationship with yourself, you will see yourself differently. Then, you prepare yourself for the opportunity to create mirror magic every time, every day you stand in front of it. The mirror can actually become a space of positive association for your Confidence Compass, your Meaningful Outcome, your motivation, and your behavior. It's an art and a science.

REFLECTION AND JOURNAL WORK

TODAY: At what times have you noticed you had self-propelling motivation?

TOMORROW: In what way was knowing yourself and valuing yourself connected to produce this motivation.

THE NEXT DAY: What is your current relationship with your mirror?

Do you look or do you see yourself? Save this reflection for your next steps.

Section III

PREPARE

10

BELIEVE IN WHO YOU SEE

"The intention of your dressing becomes the intention of your day." -MCG.

You may look at getting into your closet and shuffling through items as just an everyday task, but know how you see yourself through the mirror in the clothes and accessories you've chosen has a huge impact on your mindset—and mindset impacts your behavior. You can change what you believe about yourself when you see yourself as the person you are becoming, the person who achieves goals.

Clothing is highly metaphorical and symbolic and when matched with the idea that "seeing is believing" it holds a practical ability to help you feel confident, productive, and important. It can anchor your self-belief to your Meaningful Outcome which helps you create powerful motivated action toward carrying it out.

In a 2012 study exploring Enclothed Cognition[1], researchers found proof of the connection between wearing clothing and subsequent behavior. In the experiment, participants were split into three groups and given a white lab coat; one group wore the lab coat but was not told it's meaning, one group wore the lab coat and was told it was a doctor's coat. The third group wore the lab coat and was told it was a painter's smock.

Each of the groups were asked to perform a task. Which do you think performed the task with more attentiveness and care?

The group that was told the lab coat was a doctor's coat performed the task with the greatest excellence. The three experiments concluded that wearing a lab

1. Hajo Adam, Adam D. Galinsky, "ScienceDirect," Journal of Experimental Social Psychology Volume 48, Issue 4, July 2012, https://doi.org/10.1016/j.jesp.2012.02.008

coat increased attention. Attention did not increase when the coat was not worn or associated with a painter. Attention only increased when the coat was 1.) worn and 2.) associated with a doctor.

This study concludes how powerful it is to not just wear clothing but to wear clothing that is symbolic. The group that had attached symbolism—a doctor's coat—to the garment took on the characteristics of how they believe a doctor would perform a task.

You can use these findings to think about your own dressing behavior. It is possible to change the way you dress to change how you see yourself in the mirror. This new way of getting dressed reflects the personal symbolism of your Confidence Compass so you act more powerfully toward your Meaningful Outcome. I teach it expertly to the women in my Hue And Style® mentorship program. We spend time in the first part of their journey creating a crystal clear definition of their Confidence Compass and Meaningful Outcome then I attach that symbolism to every color, garment, and accessory they put on their body. When they dress themselves in Hue And Style®, they believe in who they see in the mirror and take massive new action from that new belief and purpose.

This new way to get dressed and prepare for your day and your life looks like this:

Seeing Is Believing

Believing Creates
Action

Motivation
Creates More Action

Action Creates
Momentum

Enthusiasm Mixed With
Purpose Produces Motivation

Momentum
Produces Enthusiasm

> Seeing is Believing → Believing Creates Action → Action Creates Momentum → Momentum Produces Enthusiasm → Enthusiasm Mixed With Purpose Produces Motivation → Motivation Creates More Action.

During times of transition, where there is an absence of personal value and a loss of meaning in your life's direction, knowing how to intentionally use the powerful symbolism of dressing to change your self-belief will help you access new resilience and confidence you didn't know you had inside.

It all starts with seeing yourself differently in the most intentional way.

When Karla came to me, she was, in her own words, "crumbling." She described herself as a shell—fragile to outside judgements and empty from past grief. She felt like one more blow to her confidence would push her past the point of recovery.

Karla is a gifted interior design technologist but at the time she came to me, she couldn't see it. She couldn't believe in her gift. All she saw when she looked in the mirror was a woman who couldn't "get it together." Her business was stagnant. She had no clients coming in and the pressure of not performing was weighing heavily on her self-belief and her relationships. She knew she needed something new inside before everything came crashing down. She thought, maybe I just need to dress better. "Look good, feel better, right?"

In our first session, Karla saw beyond just putting new shirts in her closet to the wide, beautiful horizon of what her life could look like if she embraced seeing herself as the woman she was becoming. From that moment on, Karla blossomed. With me, she found a crystal-clear definition of her Confidence Compass and Meaningful Outcome. It was powerful. The day she learned to attach symbolism to her dressing was the day I watched her take the deepest most healing breathe of liberation. She had returned to herself. From that day on, she exploded in confidence (and yes, in style), but more importantly she started showing up every day as a manifestation of her gifts, talents, virtues, values, and purpose. A wave of new momentum followed.

Only a few short months later, Karla had revived her design business, was fearless to promote herself, raised her prices and was attracting high-level clients who could fly her on their private jet to work on their project. Karla is just one example of how changing how you see yourself, attaching intentionally defined symbolism to what you wear becomes a superpower for your next level of life and success.

Years after her Hue And Style® mentorship with me, Karla continues to thrive even when faced with new changes and transitions. She continues to use the confidence mindset-shift tools anchored by her ability to honor herself every day by getting dressed in a way that changes her self-belief. It's a joy to watch part of my own Meaningful Outcome of creating permanent results in others. She is not alone. The women I mentor all own this power. Mission accomplished.

REFLECTION AND JOURNAL WORK

TODAY: Where have you found yourself stuck in the "seeing is believing" cycle?

TOMORROW: Where have you seen that your level of self-belief has stolen your ability to take action?

THE NEXT DAY: If you could get it exactly right, what would seeing yourself differently every day you get dressed help you achieve?

11

DRESS IN CONFIDENCE

"Dressing well is not about fashion or vanity. It's about self-expression, self-acceptance, self-love, and teaching others how to treat you." ~MCG .

Your dressing behavior today, right now, is a reflection of your mindset from your last transition. This starting belief affects how you see yourself, which affects your actions, momentum, enthusiasm, outcomes, and joy.

The more closets I visited in the early days of my image consultancy, the more evidence I saw of this powerful cycle. As I shifted my work, I helped more and more women trapped in crippling mindsets start to release them as they changed how they saw themselves. The beliefs keeping them stuck shifted and their self-worth climbed as they aligned their closets and dressing behavior. They felt a surge of new joy (not to mention they dressed in the best style of their lives.)

One client who stands out vividly was preparing to start her business. She always had a dream of becoming an entrepreneur, but like many who begin going out on their own she was afraid of the unknown. This transition in business was filled with uncertainty which brought up old beliefs about her ability to be successful.

Going through her closet, I found one worn out, black maternity nursing top. She stopped me with a sense of distress as I pulled it out and said, "Wait! I wear that one all the time." I looked at the garment with confusion. "Really," I said, "It's super worn out, not in your Hue And Style® color palette and looks just tired."

It was like a light bulb turned on and illuminated her face. The realization of something more was hitting her like a ton of bricks and just as it did, I asked,

"What does this top mean to you?"

She told me it was the nursing shirt she wore all the time when her son was a baby and that it was a time, she felt safe, connected, and happy because she had overcome a tough start to her breast-feeding journey. I looked in her eyes and asked, "How old is your son?"

"He's 10," she said with the shade of realization coming over her face as my jaw dropped at the same time. I gathered myself to ask the next big question,

"What do you believe about yourself right now about starting your business?"

She answered, "It's scary. I just want to feel safe and like I can do it."

And there it was. She had attached the symbolism of feeling safe and successful and the belief that she wasn't sure she could be a successful business owner to her dressing behavior.

That was the last appointment I ever did that only dealt with the clothes. From then on, I had the opportunity and privilege to help women do something so much bigger than just "styling an outfit" or cleaning out a closet. This was a *thing*. It was now going to be my mission to help them dress in confidence—to put on renewed self-belief and energized purpose every day anchored in every color, garment, and accessory—in a way that only I could.

To embrace this new awareness, take a look in your closet today. There are clues in your closet that are highlighting a current imbalance of your beliefs and priorities from your most recent transition. Remember that beauty of change? Right now, is your opportunity to discover a place of growth—inside your closet.

Think about your dressing behavior. You are needing a proven process of realignment if you:

- Wear the same thing and tell yourself you have a "fashion uniform."
- Wear clothes that are too big or too small.
- Wear all Black, White, Grey or other neutrals under the belief that it is "easy," "slimming," "always chic" or that you "just don't do color."
- Have volumes of clothes but always claiming "I have nothing to wear."

- Have clothing hanging in your closet with the tags on and having little idea of why you don't wear what you bought.
- Rush past mirrors not wanting to see yourself.

Your typical wardrobe frustrations are also a clue. Your confidence mindset needs renewing if you:

- Hate shopping because it stresses you out and you can never find anything that works.
- Have chronic disorganization in your closet or accessories leading to not knowing or forgetting what you have.
- Practice aimless seasonal purging of your closet with only a plan to "get organized" but not with a purpose to move forward.
- Go on mass shopping "hauls" yet not remembering what you bought a short time later.
- Get lost in endless inspiration gathering, "pinning," or following of bloggers and fashionistas "for ideas."
- Think intentional dressing "doesn't matter" that much because you're "just a __ (insert

role: stay at home mom, wife, teacher, nurse . . .)"

Ok, breathe. I know it's a lot and you may see more than a few of these symptoms playing out in your closet. Let me reassure you. This is not a scolding about your current state. This is a signal. You have an opportunity to shift how you see the meaning of these symptoms. These clues are not telling you that you need to purge your closet, go on a shopping haul, or find new ways to style-up your wardrobe. As an image-confidence expert, these symptoms are telling you to pay attention to the thoughts and beliefs you have related to your latest change and the transition you are experiencing.

Which are you experiencing?

- Feeling like you don't know who you are anymore
- Feeling tired, lonely or abandoned
- Feeling aimless or purposeless
- Feeling a loss of enthusiasm
- Feeling stuck or stagnant
- Feeling overwhelmed or scattered
- Feeling like you don't know your role

- Feeling like you don't belong
- Feeling unworthy in some way
- Feeling unsure in your abilities

All of these feelings show up in your closet. You now know that getting dressed is more than putting on a top and a bottom but attached to everything that is inside you. If you can now see that your closet can show you where you are stuck, I bet you can believe it can also become a source of power.

Back in high school, I was a nationally ranked debate competitor.

I was so excited to be invited to represent my province in the 1996 national high school debate championship. It was in Windsor, Ontario that year. All the best high school debate competitors from all provinces across Canada would be there. This was a big deal. It was the Olympics to me.

The second day of competition was to be a model parliament debate that mimics the lively Government and Opposition exchanges in Canada's House of Commons where debate is passionate and party lines are drawn. I had always loved parliamentary style debate and to have it organized in realistic fashion in the old limestone building of the local university made it feel so real.

The day before the model parliament, my team had a chance to prepare our strategy and arguments to a resolution. In our preparation room, my team chose me as the Leader of the Opposition—the primary speaker of our team. I accepted but was scared. Not nervous, but scared. It didn't feel like I belonged in this caliber of competitors or that I had the ability to lead the team.

That night after prep, I started thinking about all the other champions in the room—on both sides. I questioned why they chose me. I wondered if I could do this massive position justice. I went to my suitcase and looked for the most "Leader of the Opposition" thing I could wear.

I thought what most think, "Just look the part."

Picture it: a late 1990s long-line tailored blazer in bright Goldenrod Yellow with Black lapel trim and embroidered military-inspired epaulets perched on top of the shoulder—propped up by massive shoulder pads. I paired it with a black pencil skirt, black hose, and closed-toed pumps. I chose my most mini-lawyer gold-knot earrings and set out an I-mean-business red-brown lipstick.

There. Now I would at least look like the Leader of the Opposition even if I messed the rest up. I didn't mess it up though. As I walked into that model parliament ring, I commanded the room and the environment having deliberately dressed as who I needed to be at that moment and what happened was what happens when you attach the proper symbolism of how you see yourself to the behaviour you need to make—I crushed it.

Little did I know back then what I know now: that the high contrast combination of Goldenrod Yellow and Black has a very particular color psychology and values communication that worked to bolster my self-belief, to influence my team to believe in my leadership, and to intimidate the opposing team.

I also would have never known that this Parliamentary Debate would be the foreshadowing for what would become part of my Meaningful Outcome. I dressed myself in confidence right into an Opposition win of the debate which ushered in a wave of new belief in my gifts and talents leading the way for how I would create my life. There is so much power when you dress in confidence—for the present, and for the momentum it brings for your future.

When you change the meaning of getting dressed in this way, you will experience five amazing fringe benefits that boost your ability to be and do more in any area of your priorities. I felt them after Model Parliament, and you will too—when you know how. When you see yourself, and believe in yourself, present yourself with authenticity (which grows confidence), you experience more:

- **Courage:** Bravery in the face of fear that is needed to take risks and steps out of your comfort zone.

- **Enthusiasm:** Excitement connected to your spirit for how you live that is authentic and attractive to people.

- **Self-Respect:** Reverence for your value and your ability to be assertive as you teach others how to treat you.

- **Humility:** Wisdom to understand your place in the world, to stay in your lane, ask for help when you need it, and offer grace to others on their own journey.

- **Joy:** Satisfaction in the present moment and the want to give and receive a feeling of happiness that springs from what you love and believe to be true.

Changing how you get dressed for your day changes how you prepare yourself to show up. If you can embrace the idea that to "dress in confidence" means to intentionally align everything on the inside of you with everything you want to create purposefully for yourself and others, you are on the brink of accessing so much new personal power. What would you create with it? What would you pursue with it?

REFLECTION AND JOURNAL WORK

TODAY: Which dressing clues or symptoms, or both are you experiencing right now?

Which feelings are you experiencing right now related to your recent transition?

TOMORROW: Which of the five by-products of dressing in confidence do you need most to create a breakthrough toward success?

How would the others relate to it if you could capture it?

THE NEXT DAY: Revisit your reflections on the relationship with your mirror. Connect any dressing clues with how you've experienced motivation. There will be a link.

12

INVITE THE RIGHT SUPPORT

"Your relationships are a reflection of your confidence and a foreshadowing of your success." ~MCG.

In the immortal words of my hairdresser, Esther, "There is a reason and a season for every relationship." You've also probably heard that "You become like the five people you hang around."

Both are true. The people who have surrounded you up until now have gotten used to you with your set of beliefs, whatever they are. Sometimes when you make a shift to do something new, like improve your confidence, or step into new behaviors because you're learning new resilience, the relationships around you are forced to shift and change too.

The reality is, every person is on their own journey to grow and evolve. Some will be on the same path of growth at the same time as you, but many won't. People come into your life to help you see or support you to learn a Whispered Lesson. Some stay for a short time, some for longer. It's important to understand that this is all natural and normal for relationships to come, go, move, change, and shift. That doesn't mean you don't feel a sense of grief when a person goes away or that you don't feel unsettled with how the relationship ended. This is also natural and normal. You are human.

The beauty of acquiring and owning a confidence that is renewing and evolving is that you have another opportunity to learn—this time about how to recognize who is best for your season at this moment. Over the years, and helping my clients align their new confidence with how the world reacts to them, I have been able to capture a powerful way to see how the people in your life support your growth.

The Friendship Umbrella

The Friendship Umbrella is my personal framework for defining relationships that ensures you care for yourself first and that all who are invited underneath it are supportive of you living your life in a meaningful and purposeful way. I designed this framework for myself as I went through a number of relationship shifts and found it to be a miracle worker for practicing discernment and detachment, and releasing the "people pleaser" feelings that kept me feeling overwhelmed by trying to manage every single relationship from everybody else's point of view.

You can apply this Friendship Umbrella to friendships or other connected relationships to help you see which relationships to nurture and strengthen and which to release.

The Five C's of Supportive Relationships

When you think about the people in your life, there is some sort of give and take—that's a relationship. Ideally it is a reciprocal, back and forth, one. You give, they give, you get, they get and it's a "net zero" type of feeling. No one feels like they gave too much or too little. It feels smooth and balanced.

The five C's are a great way to check in to see if you are in fact involved in that kind of reciprocal feeding, nurturing relationship.

The five C's for supportive relationships are all "ch" verbs. Why? Verbs are doing words, action words, and supportive friendships happen when actions are taken time and time again between each other. The result has a positive impact on both parties.

For anyone that you would call a friend or a supportive, important relationship, these five C's need to exist. There are four basic C's and then one over-arching one (the Umbrella).

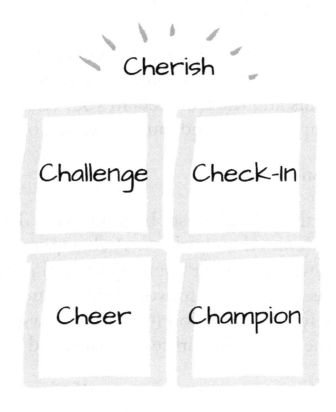

Cheer

A supportive relationship must cheer you on. To cheer means they are rooting for you. It means they clap for you. Maybe not literally, but in the sense that they are excited for your next step and encourage you to move forward. They do it privately for certain and the truest will do it publicly.

They are a cheerleader in your corner, the banner waver as you cross the finish line, they are the wind at your sails and the trumpets in your cheering section. A supportive friend must cheer you on.

Champion

A supportive friend must champion you. To champion is different than to cheer. A champion as someone who will hold your name up high in public and in private. They vouch for you, recommend you, but not only for the work you may do or how you do it but for the values and virtues you own and share.

A champion is someone that even if you don't talk to them very often, they are in the background sharing you with other people because they believe in your gifts, talents, values, and virtues and how you live to serve your Meaningful Outcome. They are behind you all the way and the truest are also your best cheerleaders.

Check-In

A supportive friend must check-in. Do they notice when you're quiet? Do they reach out to you? Do they wonder what is up? Check-ins are about the receiver, not the giver's own motivation. They are about genuinely caring to know if you are purposefully meeting your Meaningful Outcome and living from your Definition of Success.

The check-in is built on the layers before it. If someone is a champion, they know your Meaningful Outcome. If they are a cheerleader, they also know your Definition of Success. Supportive friends who check-in ask and listen about all of these and that's what makes them so powerfully valuable as a relationship.

Challenge

The fourth C gets a little tougher and is the difference between someone being an acquaintance or a nice person in your life and someone who is a catalyst for your growth. A supportive friend must challenge. Does the person challenge you to be your best? Do they challenge you to live from your Definition of Success and Meaningful Outcome every day? Do they ask you questions on it? Do they ask you to consider another way? Do they ask you about what you're doing next to fulfill it?

To challenge is tough and it requires a very specific kind of relationship. It requires a genuine interest in that person growing. When you can get to the point of being able to challenge, it is a deeper connection between two people. This connection builds a profound sense of trust and a pure sense of love and gratitude for the relationship. Challenge is the one that is the difference between simply having a nice cup-of-coffee-chat friend and having someone that moves you to another level of success.

Cherish

The last C is the umbrella. It's the one that rides above all four and that even if you have all four, if you are missing this one, something feels like it's missing. It may seem that one party takes the relationship more seriously than the other. It may seem that one side of the relationship takes advantage of the other. It's the piece where the peace and balance of a friendship resides; that is to cherish.

To cherish means to hold something sacred or special; to know that if it was gone from your life you would miss it dearly, deeply, emotionally, and longingly—that you would grieve it. To cherish something means you hold deep love for it where there is no envy, or comparison, where there is no need to feel esteemed above or below one another—you are equal—no matter where the relationship goes there can always be mending and healing because it's cherished by both. These friends love to be in your space, and they feel blessed to be in it. They see you as a gift in their life and the feeling is mutual.

You will have a range of different relationships in your life right now based on how many of these C's a person holds for you. You may be surprised when you look at the people around you who have all five and who does not. You may find placing your relationships on the framework helps make sense of how they have come into or left your life. Hidden gems may come out of nowhere with all five, while people you expect to have it all don't—and you can see why there is tension. The five Cs are my gift to you to help you find new perspectives in your relationships.

When you surround yourself with the right types of relationships, your confidence grows like wildfire and your ability to summon your resilience explodes. If you have people who cheer on, who champion who you are, and your Meaningful Outcome, who challenge you to always be moving forward in it in purpose, who check in and make sure you're going in the right direction and who cherish every single second they can spend with you and watch you grow and become the person you are meant to be, you can't help but transform.

My dear client turned friend, Vivian, was one of my first image consulting clients. She's a caretaker and a caregiver having looked after her aging parents until their passing and other aging relatives while working full-time as a non-profit executive director. Needless to say, she was busy when we met.

The work we shared together in aligning her image and confidence was, in her words, "soul-saving" she told me after our consultant/client relationship turned to a friendship. She said to me one day, "Michele, these women listening to you from afar don't know how valuable what you teach in mentorship is. They think it's just about clothes or one color but what I've learned from you is to believe in myself to take on any situation, in the face of any judgement. I've repaired my relationship with myself and learned not to compromise it for anyone. It's power and it's permanent."

Vivian shared this after attending a family wedding where strained relationships were put to the test as they were all put in a room together.

She told me, "Michele, in my previous life, before the confidence you taught me, I never would have gone. I would have stayed at home fearful of what they would say about me, my actions, and the way I live my life. Instead, I was able to arrive at the spot, not attached to any judgment of anyone who would be outside myself. I walked in my power, looking amazing by the way, understood my reason for being there, greeted the people that I needed to, and left when I felt compelled to—assertive—with no guilt, shame, regret, or burden. It could have been the most difficult day, but it wasn't thanks to the lessons I learned from your mentorship.

What Vivian experienced was the power of self-work, self-belief, alignment of relationships for her resilience and living from the truest place. In that place, you are very much enough. In that place, relationships become enhancements, not burdens and you're able to choose, nurture or release them as needed. That's true liberation.

Supercharge Your Success with Mentorship

In any area you want to improve, there are critical elements you don't know. There are two gaps that exist between who you are today and what you want to grow into tomorrow. There will always be a knowledge gap and a mindset gap. One or both of these will keep you stuck where you are until your current situation is annoying enough, unbearable enough, or dire enough to take action to close those two gaps.

One of the fastest ways to close that gap is through a mentorship relationship. Mentorship is a special relationship between two people. One knows more than the other, has gotten where the other desires to be and there is a special bond for the mentor to want to get the mentee to their next step.

In the best mentorship realms, both the mentor and mentee are fulfilled by a reciprocal relationship. The mentor feels happiness and satisfaction to move the mentee through their knowledge and mindset gaps with their insight and support; and the mentee feels liberated and powerful to grow and achieve their outcome applying what they have learned.

There is an important component that makes mentorship different from other helping relationships. The best mentors are:

- Interested in a long-term solution over a short-term outcome focused on the "who" you are becoming over the "what" you are achieving knowing that the "who" of stronger character, definition and confidence will always create the "what."
- Connected to your limiting beliefs that would hold you back from closing the knowledge and mindset gaps. They feel a responsibility to call you on them and can because the depth of the relationship has implicit trust.

These components form a true mentorship relationship experience that lifts you and creates results you could never have imagined. Miss one of these pieces and you will have one of three things:

- A teacher
- A friend
- An inspiration

These roles are all needed in our lives. They all serve a purpose. You can be inspired and relate to a person as an expert or as someone you look up to but they are only a mentor of yours once you have a relationship with them and they have a relationship with you based on close trust. They've been where you want to go, they are able to take you there and you are open, willing, and invested to follow their lead. That's how you get to skyrocket your way to live out your Meaningful Outcome, a mentor will be priceless.

How to Find a Mentor

Being a mentor and a mentee is a back and forth, reciprocal, relationship. Before seeking mentorship, you want to know a few things about yourself. You will want to know:

- The exact outcome you desire. What do you want to feel happy and fulfilled? What are you missing in knowledge and mindset that are keeping you from getting to where you desire?
- An idea of the limiting beliefs holding you back. You may not know exactly how to articulate them but having an idea of what has stopped you in the past will be a starting point. A good mentor will be able to see it, name it and offer you clarity around it.

Once you know these about yourself, you can now seek a mentor who can help you with your growth and achievement. You may have someone in mind, or you may simply put these characteristics in your mind and begin seeking ideas. The mentor right for you:

- Embodies the character you wish to develop or strengthen. This doesn't mean personality expression, this means the qualities of gifts, talent, virtue and values.
- Has achieved the exact outcome you wish for yourself and is willing to walk you to it.

Choose your mentor always based first on the character you want to emulate, then on the outcome they can help you achieve. You'll know when it resonates with you—it will be a gut feeling, a warm feeling or a feeling like you've known them forever even if you've just met.

After you have decided who you think would be a great mentor, you need to start a relationship with them to be sure you have a fit and that they want to mentor you. Remember it is a reciprocal relationship—a two-way street—where both parties receive satisfaction and fulfillment. It is not a relationship done without conversations about dreams, aims, your Meaningful Outcome as well as your limiting beliefs and roadblocks.

There are a few ways to see if you have a fit to establish a mentoring relationship:

- Ask to meet them, on a phone call or apply to work with them.
- Be upfront with what you're seeking. Let them know why you see them as a possible mentor for you.
- Understand that they need to see a fit too

since mentoring may be part of their professional expertise or offerings.

- Be confident enough to know they may give you criteria in order for them to come alongside you or that they may not be able to take on the relationship for their own reasons.

Sometimes mentorship relationships happen more organically and may start as a paid coaching experience that evolves from a business relationship, employee-boss ties or networking opportunities. These can be helpful connections just keep in mind for them to be fruitful mentoring connections, they need to have the right start, characteristics and outcomes.

Done in the most heart-filling way, mentorship relationships will all five C's layered with an extra dose of love. They can be life-long, cherished parts of your life making them absolutely priceless.

I was told early in my business career to find a mentor who has the exact outcome you desire. Be sure you have a fit and then do whatEVER it takes to work with them. You will never regret it and the time, effort, and any investment as it will come back to you

1000-fold.

Having powerfully fulfilling friendships and mentorship relationships puts wind in your sails for accelerated personal growth. Never underestimate the power of understanding why you have the people in your life that you do. Review their position regularly because it will change over time. Audit their involvement in your life accordingly because you will need to let some go and invite others closer. And when you need to release a relationship, do it with loving kindness. Honor the place they held in your life at the season you needed it and look forward to your next horizon knowing your renewal will offer more to the people who will support your next steps.

REFLECTION AND JOURNAL WORK

TODAY: Assess the friendships you spend the most time with in this new way. What are your insights about each?

TOMORROW: Assess any relationships that are challenged right now. Where do they fit?

Can you see a connection or disconnection between what you need and what they are offering?

THE NEXT DAY: Think about how you want to honor the special relationships that fill all five areas. Consider how you want to address those that are challenged.

*Bonus Reflection:

Explore if you have a mentor or mentors in your life. Who are they?

What characteristics do they have?

If you don't have one, think about what area of your life you could use this kind of deep and meaningful relationship.

13

GET READY TO SHOW UP

"Healing is the aim. Freedom is the dream." ~MCG.

As you take your journey, there will be times where what is happening inside you doesn't make sense, it feels itchy, sticky or rough. Watch, listen and learn. Here are some of my insights to inspire you to remember that what is happening on the inside is a setup for your next breakthrough:

You serve more people than you know by simply being you.

There is no one like you. There is no one who has the collection of gifts, talents, virtues and values as you. No one. You have a purpose here and it's only to live out the expression of your Meaningful Outcome. Focus on keeping it in front of you every step of your life.

In tears there's truth.

Cry. It is a beautiful signal that you are as close to the heart of your feelings as you can be. Instead of pushing it down, trying to turn them off, focus on what they are sharing with you. There is a truth to your growth and your lesson. Find meaning in them. Name the feeling they represent, release judgement about it, and honor it: relief, joy, grief, excitement, love. There is truth in your tears. Don't stop crying until you know what it is.

Write until your hand hurts.

The voice of your true self sounds so much different in tone and language than the voice of the outside world influencing you. It can take a while to get used to hearing it. It can take a few pages to hear it whisper but when you do, every good idea, every supportive tidbit is revealed to you. You just have to ask. Write until your hand hurts. Sometimes it's after one page, sometimes it's after four when you feel that hand start to ache you're in the right place. Start listening.

When the world is loud, create your own peace.

We all get overwhelmed.? The causes may be different, the circumstances may be varied but we ALL have times of overwhelm. That's when the world seems to get loud. Have you noticed it? When you do, find your peace. Peace means different things to everyone. Not always a place of quiet but always a place of joy. It could be when you shovel freshly fallen snow with good reggae music in your ears. Peace.? It could be doodling with no agenda. Peace. It could be sipping the hottest dark roast coffee. Peace. Explore where you find your Peace. Go there today.

Confidence is self-love in action.

To use change to move you forward with confidence needs renewed self-love. You find it in the private moments where you are vulnerable with yourself, where you see new clarity. The confidence to take new action is your new self-love working for you. Focus quietly on yourself.

You are being prepared for a success you can't yet see.

Right now, life is preparing you with experience and lessons for your next step. "Preparation" is not only about skills, but also about making your heart and mind ready to use those skills. Your preparation is about seeing your value, finding new self-love, and accepting that confidence is not something you get and then just have—a destination. The confidence you'll need for success is always evolving through your preparation. Commit to a journey.

The intention of your dressing becomes the intention of your day.

As you choose what to put on tomorrow, as you head into new ways to create success this week, consider if you see yourself in the mirror. Learn to make what you see intentional, expressive, symbolic and above all else, meaningful. When you do, you will be beyond simply stylish, you will be powerfully change-making. #GetUpAndDressed

Replace your worries with your good work.

There's a difference between doing work and doing the good work. Work gets things done. The good work changes things. Work feels like grinding. The good work sparks the feels. Work has a goal to finish. The good work's goal is to transform. Work is what you do every day. The good work is every day loving what you do. When you do the good work, worry fades away. There's no space for it. Focus on making whatever you do today meaningful. Focus on your good work.

Take uncomfortable and inconvenient action.

The opportunities that have the power to change you deeply, will feel uncomfortable and inconvenient. You will question if you are worth it, if you can make it happen, if you have what it takes or if it will be worth it. It will be if you stick to it because the opportunities that come to you are testing your confidence and resilience. See the lesson. Work it and wait for your blessing.

Balance the doing with the feeling.

Creating success that makes you fulfilled and joyful every day and happy to show up and claim your space is about balancing the "feeling" you get from your definition of success with the "doing" of creating it. No one can define this mix for you. No one can be sure you're preparing yourself to truly live it—only you can do that. Check in daily.

Connect with those who see your light and celebrate your flame.

Many may see your light but not all will celebrate your flame. [Pause on that.] Connect with those who not only 'see you' but champion you. Cherish them. They are wind in your sails for growth. They are essential for your next success. Share with them your gratitude.

A little belief breathed into someone goes a long way.

If you ever lose your Meaningful Outcome for a split second, just do this. It's enough to refresh your hope and find your new path.

Trust your gut. Pivot quickly. Have faith in your choices and wait for your perfect outcome.

Rinse and repeat. That is all.

Your legacy lives in those you change.

Your only responsibility is to create your own legacy. The indelible impression you leave on the lives of people you change with your Meaningful Outcome will be a wave that ripples out generations. Be a drop in the lives of those you change. Be content in that the ripple will live on.

You will change the world with your confidence.

When you have the sureness of self, you can do anything.

You say "yes" when you want to.

You say "no" when you need to.

You give when you can't.

You give more when you can.

You stand up when you are compelled.

You sit down when you are ready.

Your words speak.

Your work speaks louder.

You share yourself.

But oh, what you share is for others.

When you have the sureness of self,

that's confidence,

you change the world.

"Sharp as a tack!"

My dad used to exclaim when we were looking dressed, ready to show up.

I now know that this exclamation means so much more than just dressing. It means:

- Owning the boldness to no longer be invisible.
- Being intentional with your actions that help people want to trust and engage with you.
- Knowing with complete self-assuredness that every choice you make—what business to build, what new skill to learn, what gig to take, what personal brand reputation to cultivate, what client to turn away, or anything else—aligns with your self-worth and values.

To be "sharp as a tack" means you live your life with purpose and show up for it ready to change yourself and those meant for your influence.

YOU ARE READY.

To see yourself as who you are becoming next is a magically powerful practice. You build this magic every day you see your life as a gift here to coax out your brilliance. As you embark and allow it to show you the way, I have a last message for you:

You will make mistakes.

You will get things wrong.

You will hurt others' feelings.

It's unavoidable you are learning the lessons of life.

See the golden opportunity.

Keep watch, listen and learn.

For each tiny step or misstep,

Course correct for a giant leap.

Keep your head on your shoulders.

Keep your wits about you.

Be prepared to use some grit and to give yourself lots of grace.

As you learn to navigate using the brilliant parts that make you, you.

You are gifted.

You are talented.

You are led by values.

You are guided by virtues.

Every time you wake and meet the day, honor these with purpose and practice—symbolically and metaphorically.

See yourself differently and watch yourself change into an individual ready to use their best to deliver what is meaningful for themselves to express in their life.

Fuel your life with purpose.

Show up with presence.

Present yourself with confidence.

Assume your authority.

Illuminate your influence.

You are powerful beyond belief.

You are everlasting in those you change.

Make your mark.

"There ain't no time to waste."

Now it's up to you. The time is now.

You simply need to decide, commit, and enjoy.

It's time to begin your journey.

It's time to:

SHOW UP CONFIDENT.

THANK YOU!

I'm sending sincere gratitude to you for reading my book and trusting me with a piece of your growth.

I love hearing what you've learned with me.

Please leave me a helpful review on Amazon letting me know what you thought of the book and what it sparked in you.

Again, many thanks!

MCg

Michele Charles Gustafson

YOU'RE INVITED TO DISCOVER MORE

If you are excited for your next step in your confidence journey, especially learning to connect it to your personal image, I am going to give you access to free resources and training along with an opportunity to join my free private community. You'll learn:

The Secrets To Changing The Way You Get Dressed
(that makes you fearless, magnetic and ready for anything)

https://www.hueandstyle.com/free-resources

Acknowledgements

I must offer my gratitude to people who helped this work come to life:

Tiffany Clarke Harrison – Developmental Editor

Andrea C. Jasmin – Copy & Proofreading Editor

Robyn Beiker – Cover Design Consultant

Leon Brown – Promotions Consultant

Ken Teramura – Challenger & Cheerleader

Chris Gustafson – Cherished Cheerleader, Champion & Challenger